MOUNT VERNON

AMERICAN LANDMARKS

Jason Cooper

The Rourke Corporation, Inc.
Vero Beach, Florida 32964

© 1999 The Rourke Corporation, Inc.

All rights reserved. No part of this book may be reproduced or utilized in any form or by any means, electronic or mechanical including photocopying, recording, or by any information storage and retrieval system without permission in writing from the publisher.

PHOTO CREDITS:
© Gene Ahrens: cover, pages 7, 10; © Breck Kent: page 13; courtesy of The Mount Vernon Ladies' Association: title page, pages 4, 8, 12, 15, 17, 18, 21

CREATIVE SERVICES:
East Coast Studios, Merritt Island, Florida

EDITORIAL SERVICES:
Susan Albury

Library of Congress Cataloging-in-Publication Data

Cooper, Jason, 1942-
    Mount Vernon / by Jason Cooper
      p. cm. — (American Landmarks)
    Includes index.
    Summary: Describes the history, original uses, and preservation of Mount Vernon, the plantation home of George Washington.
    ISBN 0-86593-548-3
    1. Mount Vernon (Va. : Estate) Juvenile literature. 2. Washington, George, 1732-1799—Homes and haunts—Virginia—Fairfax County Juvenile literature. [1. Mount Vernon (Va. : Estate) 2. Washington, George, 1732-1799—Homes and haunts.] I. Title. II. Series: Cooper, Jason, 1942- American landmarks.
E312.5.C66 1999
975.5'291—dc21   99-27475
                                                                               CIP

Printed in the USA

TABLE OF CONTENTS

Mount Vernon	5
The General at Mount Vernon	9
Life at Mount Vernon	14
Washington the Farmer	19
The Mansion	20
Visiting Mount Vernon	22
Glossary	23
Index	24
Further Reading	24

MOUNT VERNON

Mount Vernon was the home and property of George Washington. Mount Vernon lies on a hilltop overlooking the Potomac River in Virginia.

George Washington was the United States's first president. He was also the general who led the untested Continental Army in its war for freedom against Great Britain.

The story of Mount Vernon itself began in 1674. The land was a gift to George's great grandfather. George, born in 1732, spent some of his boyhood at Mount Vernon.

Most of the Mount Vernon mansion was built by Augustine Washington, George Washington's father, who lived here in the 1730s.

In 1754 he **leased** (LEESSD) Mount Vernon from the widow of his half-brother, Lawrence Washington. It was Lawrence who had begun calling the home and property Mount Vernon. Lawrence had served in the British navy under Admiral Edward Vernon. The property had been known as Little Hunting Creek Plantation before that.

Over the years, George Washington was away from Mount Vernon far more than he wished. But he was very busy doing the work of the new nation.

During the eight years he was president (1789-1797), he visited Mount Vernon just 15 times.

Augustine Washington's home was a one-half story building. General Washington added a full story to the house before his marriage to Martha Custis in 1759.

THE GENERAL AT MOUNT VERNON

Before he was general, George Washington was an aide to General Edward Braddock from 1752 until 1759. In those days, Americans and British soldiers fought together against the French. As a soldier, Washington did not often visit Mount Vernon.

Washington left the army in 1759, and he married Martha Custis that year. The Washingtons moved to Mount Vernon.

In 1761 Lawrence Washington's widow, the owner of Mount Vernon, died. George and Martha Washington became the new owners.

George Washington maintained many gardens at Mount Vernon. He left his farms and gardens in 1775 to become commander-in-chief of the Continental Army.

Washington became commander of the new Continental Army in 1775. He had a huge job—to lead his little Continental Army against the might of Great Britain. With the help of France, Washington got the job done.

For the better part of eight years (1775-1783), the general was away from Mount Vernon, fighting the British and helping found the new nation. In 1783, Washington retired to Mount Vernon briefly.

In 1789 Washington was elected the first president of the United States. Again, Washington left Mount Vernon behind to serve his country. He returned in 1797, but died in 1799.

Daffodils and tulips bloom in the spring at Mount Vernon. One of the general's gardens was for his experiments with plants.

Copies of this painting of Mount Vernon in George Washington's time were sold by the Mount Vernon Ladies' Association to raise money for the property.

The remains of General Washington and his wife lie in this tomb, built in 1831, at Mount Vernon. White marble statues nearby are memorials to other family members.

LIFE AT MOUNT VERNON

Mount Vernon was like a village, or group of villages. The 8,000 acres (3,239 hectares) of the **plantation** (plan TAY shun) were divided into five smaller farms. Each farm had its own buildings, equipment, and animals. Almost everything the plantation needed was produced on it.

Like other southern plantations of the time, Mount Vernon's human labor was provided by slaves. Slaves served as gardeners, shoemakers, bricklayers, painters, cooks, **coachmen** (KOHCH min), plowmen, maids, pickers, and **seamstresses** (SEEM struhss iss).

This is the interior of a slave hut in the greenhouse area of Mount Vernon.

Washington had about 20 working slaves when he started farming at Mount Vernon in 1758. At his death, he had more than 200 working slaves.

George Washington had been born into a system of slavery. As he aged, his feelings about slavery changed. He wrote that he was "against this kind of traffic in the human species." His will freed his slaves a year after his death.

Washington wished that Virginia, his home state, would gradually do away with slavery. However, it took another war, the Civil War (1861-1865), to make that wish come true.

Washington's storehouse at Mount Vernon still contains many of the shovels, field tools, pans, barrels, and powder horns that the general used.

WASHINGTON THE FARMER

George Washington loved to farm. For the times, he was a very modern, skilled farmer. He tried new ideas. He stayed in touch with the leading farmers of England. He practiced **crop rotation** (KRAHP ro TAY shun) which meant leaving some fields unplanted.

Washington was an expert horseman. He kept fine horses, but he also experimented with the use of donkeys and mules.

Washington had a greenhouse and several gardens. He built a 16-sided, nearly round barn, perfect for horses to **tread** (TRED) wheat.

Several of the plates and other utensils in the mansion kitchen were used by General and Mrs. Washington.

THE MANSION

   The 500 acres (200 hectares) around Washington's home, the **mansion** (MANT shun), became known as the Mansion House Farm.

   The mansion at Mount Vernon is a wonderful example of how big plantation homes looked in the 1700s. Washington himself helped design the mansion.

   In 1858 Mount Vernon was bought by the Mount Vernon Ladies' Association. The Washington family could no longer keep up the property. Neither the United States Government nor the state of Virginia showed interest in buying the property.

This is the west parlor of the mansion. The Washingtons often entertained guests in this formal room.

VISITING MOUNT VERNON

The Mount Vernon Ladies' Association bought Mount Vernon to preserve it for all Americans. About 1,000,000 visitors come to Mount Vernon each year.

Visitors tour the grounds and mansion. The great 16-sided barn has been rebuilt to match the first. Costumed workers help re-create plantation life.

Many special activities are held. In February, for example, visitors learn more about the life of plantation slaves during Black History Month.

By saving Mount Vernon, the MVLA helped save a special place in American history.

GLOSSARY

coachmen (KOHCH min) — those who drive horse-pulled coaches or carriages

colony (KAH luh nee) — a place settled by people who keep ties to their former nation; a place apart from but ruled by the nation that started it

crop rotation (KRAHP ro TAY shun) a farming method in which the crops planted in a field are changed from year to year and in some years the field is left unplanted

leased (LEESSD) — rented for a long period

mansion (MANT shun) — a large, impressive house

plantation (plan TAY shun) — a large farm or estate, usually run by people living on the farm

seamstress (SEEM struhss) one who sews or makes clothes

tread (TRED) to trample, especially for the purpose of breaking open wheat kernels

INDEX

Army, Continental   5, 8, 9, 11
barn   19, 22
Black History Month   22
Braddock, Edward General   9
Civil War   16
donkeys   19
farmers   19
farms   14
gardens   10, 19
Great Britain   5, 11
horses   18, 20, 21, 22
Mansion House Farm   20
Mount Vernon Ladies,
    Association   13, 20, 22
mules   19
plantation   14, 22
Potomac River   5
slavery   14, 15, 16
soldiers   9
Vernon, Admiral Edward   6
Virginia   5, 16, 20
Washington, Augustine   4, 7
Washington, George   4, 5, 6, 7, 8, 9, 12
Washington, Lawrence   6, 9
Washington, Martha Custis   7, 9, 12

FURTHER READING
Find out more about Mount Vernon and George Washington with these helpful books:
- Giblin, James Cross. *George Washington, A Picture Book Biography.* Scholastic, 1992.
- Gross, Ruth Belov. *If You Grew Up with George Washington.* Scholastic, 1982.
- Heilbroner, Joan. *Meet George Washington.* Random House, 1984.
- Krull, Kathleen. *Lives of the Presidents*. Harcourt Brace, 1998.